GW00818440

Totton and surroundings
in old picture postcards

by Patrick Swadling

European Library ZALTBOMMEL / THE NETHERLANDS

GB ISBN 90 288 6308 7

© 1996 European Library – Zaltbommel/The Netherlands

Introduction

As this is a book of old picture postcards, a brief look at their history would perhaps help to show how the hobby of collecting postcards first started.

Picture postcards first appeared in Austria in 1869. By the early 1900s the British had really taken this method of sending messages to each other seriously and soon what is known as the 'Golden Age' of the postcard had arrived. Everybody sent postcards, it was cheap – the postage rate was only a halfpenny – and it was reliable. Often cards were posted in the morning to arrange a meeting in the afternoon with the recipient. Publishers flourished, and cards were produced in their millions. Everyone collected picture postcards, which were then proudly put into special albums. Get togethers were arranged to show friends and neighbours new acquisitions to the collection, and woe betide the person who went on holiday and did not send back a 'Wish you were here' card to family and friends.

Suddenly local professional photographers realised here was a potentially lucrative market for their work, so off they went with their large, cumbersome plate cameras and photographed every local event of importance, from the crowning of the May Queen to the funeral of a well-loved vicar.

But they didn't stop there, every road and by-way was also photographed, even individual houses, often to order, so the cards could be sent as Christmas cards by the occupier. It is said that somewhere there is a postcard of every street in Britain. These old postcards, however, are not just a view of some long forgotten event or vanished street scene, they are a window on a way of life which will never return. They are, indeed, an important photographic social and historical record.

This book then, is a picture postcard record of the life of Totton and its surrounding villages, of Eling, Hounsdown, Netley Marsh, Redbridge and the people who lived and worked in them. It is a glimpse of a life lived at a more leisurely pace, where the sound of a horse and cart and the blacksmiths anvil were part of everyday life.

This is my second book of old postcards in the European Library series. The first was ten years ago, and has become, like the postcards themselves, something of a collector's item. This second book contains many 'new' cards, but it does not aspire to offer a history of the villages shown, because most of these areas have already been covered by other far more knowledgeable authors than myself. Totton and Eling Historical Society in particular have issued a number of excellent studies.

This book is dedicated to all those kind people who have urged, encouraged and helped me to go into print again. It has been my pleasure. Finally my thanks must go to Mr. Mike Coffin, who reproduced all the photographs.

1   In the early 1900s Rumbridge Street, Totton, must have been one of the busiest and most photographed streets in Totton. This is another wonderful piece of local social history. The building on the right was the St. Mary's Mission, sometimes called the Chapel of Ease.

2   Rumbridge Street, Totton.
A splendid view, looking
along Rumbridge Street towards Batts Corner. There is
no date on the card, but it's
probably early 1900s.

RUMBRIDGE STREET, TOTTON.

Hobbs Series. 5

3   A very early view of
Rumbridge Street, Totton,
published in the famous
F.G.O. Stuart postcard series.

Rumbridge Street, Totton.   Hants.

4　There are many 'good' postcards of Rumbridge Street, Totton, this one though surely earns its place in any pictorial history of the area. Certainly there is no hint of the volume of traffic using the road today.

5   A more unusual view of Commercial Road, Totton. The butcher's shop, P. Sutton, has now made way for a branch of Lloyds Bank.

6   A 'classic' street scene of Commercial Road, Totton. The shops are all still there and still busy. One of the first shops to open is on the left, the locally well-known Cards fish shop. The traffic has increased considerably though since this picture was taken.

7 The corner of Rumbridge Street, Totton. This side of the street does not seem to have been photographed so often, but this is a cracking view, showing as it does the old forge behind the group of children. The forge has long since gone, and there are certainly no horse-drawn carts now.

Totton.

Mentor & Co

8   Another super postcard of Totton High Street. The house on the left-hand side of the street has now been demolished to make room for a Department of Social Security building.

9   Situated on the corner of Rumbridge Street and Eling Lane, this was perhaps one of the best-known shops in Totton. It was owned and run by the three Miss Batts. The card is dated 1926.

10   The High Street, Totton.
This street was one of
Totton's main shopping
centres and included a bakery,
a milliner's and a newsagent's.

HIGH STREET, TOTTON.

11   No book of picture postcards of Totton would be complete without this view of the High Street. Note the advertisement for Ashby's Eling Brewery Company on the side of the Swan Inn.

12   High Street, Totton.
There have been several
changes on this corner of the
High Street. The building on
the corner was originally the
shop of Mr. C.F. Read, boot-
and shoemaker; later it became a branch of Lloyds
Bank, and is now a successful
dance school. It is most un-
likely that the lamp-post
would survive long in today's
traffic.

13 One of the few early views of Junction Road, Totton. It is now a very busy road. Some of the houses have been converted into shops and offices.

14   The Schools, Totton, is instantly recognisable as Eling Infant School. The school celebrated its centenary in 1995 with numerous events, including all the children and teachers dressing up in Victorian costumes.

15 This is Eling Lane, Totton, a true peep into the quiet leisurely times of years past. A fascinating picture this, as very few views of Eling Lane exist.

ELING LANE, TOTTON.

16   The Anchor Inn at Eling, Totton. This public house dates from at least the 18th century; in those days it was patronised by both local people and crews from visiting ships. Today the Anchor Inn is still popular with its customers, who now include the yachtsmen and women whose boats are moored at Eling Quay. The card is post-marked June 1913.

THE ANCHOR. ELING.

17   Eling Mills, Totton. The large building with the tower was Mumford's Steam Mill, which, with Eling Tide Mill, was one of a series of mills in the area at that time. The steam mill was eventually destroyed by fire in 1966. The site now houses the new Totton Museum.

ELING MILLS TOTTON 7

18   Paying the toll at Eling Mill, Totton. Although obviously posed, as a piece of social history this picture is irreplaceable. A right to levy tolls on vehicles crossing the causeway at Eling has been in existence for at least two hundred years, and a charge is still in place today. There were originally six tollgates in or around Totton.

"THE TOLL GATE" ELING MILL.

19   Eling Causeway, Totton, looking from the mill towards Eling Church. On the right you can see the controls to the sluice gates. The bungalow on the left is still there, but has altered in appearance.

Eling Causeway. Southampton

20   A superb view of Eling Church, Totton. Pictured in the early 1900s, it shows the houses on the right which were demolished some years ago.

21   Eling Church, Totton, was photographed inside and out from every conceivable angle. Postmarked 1907 this very early picture was taken before the installation of the rood-screen. These interior pictures have assumed great historical importance, as all the pews have now been removed and replaced by chairs.

22   Another view of the interior of Eling Church. Clearly showing the church organ, which as part of a recent refurbishment has been moved to another part of the church.

INTERIOR. TOTTON CHURCH . COPYRIGHT.   2

23 An interesting view of the rear of Eling Church, Totton, taken from Goatee (incorrect spelling on the card). Goatee Beach is the only place from where you can see all seven crosses on Eling Church simultaneously.

24 A 1910 postcard giving
a flavour of just how busy
Eling Quay was at that time,
with the masted ships loading
and unloading.

25   A pleasant picture of Eling Quay, Totton, looking particularly peaceful. Nowadays it is a hive of activity, with boat owners busy working on their vessels.

26   This happy scene was taken in 1911 at Goatee Beach, Eling, Totton. Regattas such as this one were very popular events, and obviously held on very hot summer days if the parasols and straw hats are anything to go by. Note also, the absence of cranes in the background, which are now accepted as part of the scenery.

27   This could easily have been an early advertising postcard for Spooner and Bailey. In fact, it is their letterhead, dated 1899. The company had their premises at Eling Quay, Totton, hence Eling Church and the shipping incorporated into the design.

28 A unique postcard of Downs Park Road, near Eling, Totton, taken in about 1930. Very few early photographs of this area seem to have survived.

29   A superb postcard of Fishers Road, Totton, post-marked 1913. The road is little changed, apart from being considerably busier. Indeed it is difficult to believe that children could play in the middle of any of Totton's roads, with so little risk from traffic.

30 Fishers Road (now Winsor Road), Totton. This road's main claim to fame in the area appears on the left: Totton Picture Theatre. The date is about 1920s.

FISHER'S ROAD, TOTTON. HOBBS' SERIES. 6

31 This Christmas greetings card needed considerable research. It was addressed to a Miss May Oram, Bartram Road, Totton, and postmarked Totton, 23 December 1913. So, where in Totton was the picture taken? It proved to be Fishers Road. It must have been taken specially for the family to send to friends and relatives as their very own personalised Christmas card. It would be fascinating to know who the two ladies and the four girls in their best dresses were. The card is signed 'N.J.R.'.

32   Bartram Road, Totton. Altough a side road, it seemed to appeal to the local photographers, as several different views of the road exist. A good example this, without a car in sight.

33   This view of Bartram Road dates from about 1910, and shows the road before it was properly made up with pavements. At that time, of course, there was no by-pass cutting across and it was possible to see Ashby's Brewery in Rumbridge Street.

BARTRAM ROAD, TOTTON.   Hobbs Series. 8

34   A rather splendid view of Station Road, Totton. This is one of the well-known Hobbs series of postcards. The building at the end is the Red Lion Hotel.

STATION ROAD, TOTTON.

35 The Red Lion public house, Totton. It is still very popular, but has undergone considerable modernisation. The thatched cottage to the left was demolished many years ago.

36 A rather nice close-up view of a crowded Totton Railway Station, taken about 1910. It is, of course, still a very busy station.

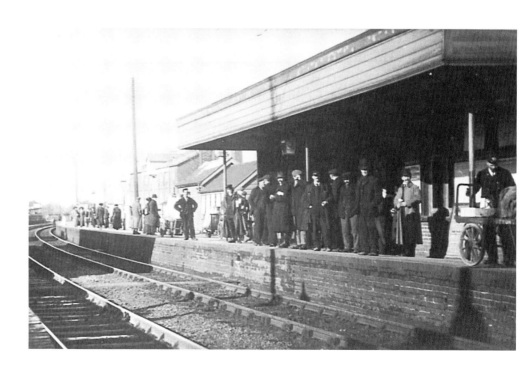

37 Totton Railway Station again, but this time a 'wide-angle' view. The large building to the right is Mumford's flour mill. The signal box in the far distance has now gone and automatic barriers control the flow of traffic through Junction Road.

38 Otter hounds at Rumbridge, Totton. This picture endorses my view that old picture postcards are important social history documents. It looks rather as if it was something of a village outing to watch the otter hounds working.

OTTER HOUNDS AT RUMBRIDGE.

39   This second view of the otter hounds at Rumbridge gives confirmation of the location. The wall the beaters are leaning against is still there. Unfortunately neither card is postmarked, so they cannot be positively dated, nor have I been able to find anyone who remembers the hunts taking place, but it must have been in the early 1900s.

40   A wider view of Rum-
bridge, Totton, where the
otter hunting took place.

Rumbridge Street, Totton, nr. Southampton.

41 Ringwood Road, Totton. A wonderfully tranquil picture. It is difficult to imagine from looking at this classic village scene that Ringwood Road is now one of the main roads from Southampton to the west.

42   Sutton Road, Testwood, Totton. Many cards by local photographers were only produced in very small numbers, and this was one of them. Very few cards are known to exist of the sideroads at Testwood.

43 Ringwood Road, Totton. This splendid picture shows the Primitive Methodist Chapel which opened in 1855. It has now taken on a new lease of life and plays an important part in the community as the Churches Together in Totton Christian Drop-in Centre.

44   This scene of the World Stores at the junction of Ringwood Road and Salisbury Road has changed out of all recognition. The stores were demolished to make room for a roundabout (Asda Roundabout), and the houses on the right were demolished to allow the Totton precinct to be built.

SALISBURY ROAD TOTTON 12

45 Salisbury Road, Totton. Very few early photographs are known of this road. This card is undated, but must be very early as the road looks little more than a wide track.

46   Another peaceful view of Salisbury Road, Totton, very different from the busy highway this road has now become. The date is early 1900s.

47 A lovely picture of what was then one of Totton's country lanes. Almost hidden in the trees, is the church of St. Anne's, Calmore. Recently extended, St. Anne's is still thriving as part of the Totton Team Ministry.

5 CALMORE CHURCH

48   Testwood Bridge, Totton. Testwood Mill was one of several mills in the area. Known as the salmon leap it was very much a local beauty spot. The River Test on which the mill still stands is famous for its excellent fishing.

49　The Salmon Pool, Test-
wood Mill, taken from a different angle. The view has
changed very little over the
years.

50 This postcard is a wonderful piece of social history. A very early picture of A. Dance and Sons', bakers, delivery cart, photographed in Rumbridge Street, Totton. The houses in the background are still there. Dance and Sons' shop was in Junction Road, later it became Lowmans. The actual bakery was in Ringwood Road, Totton.

51 A charabanc belonging to the then well-known Totton company of Tombs and Drake. Everyone seemed to visit Gough Caves at Cheddar in those days. The postcard is undated, but probably from the 1920s.

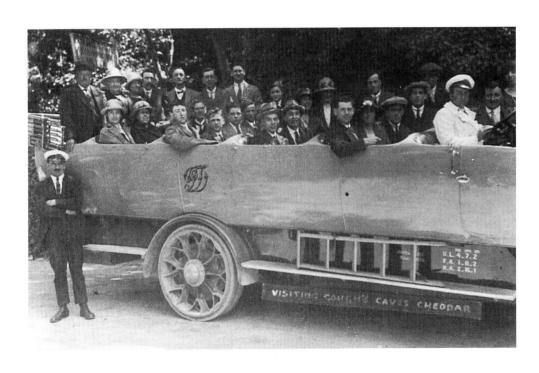

52 No explanation is needed for this wonderful card, except to say T. Burt's motor business has long since disappeared. The building, though, still stands on the corner of Station Road and Commercial Road, Totton.

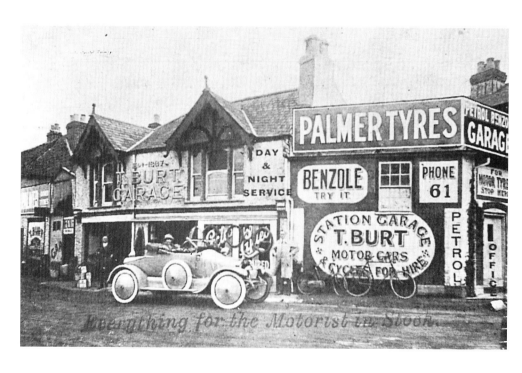

53   One of the many floats which took part in the peace celebrations at Totton, 1918. Totton Scout troop were very much involved.

54 Novelty postcards are plentiful, except for those containing views of Totton. The basket 'hides' a string of miniature views of Totton.

Two
"Small Scotches" from TOTTON

Two trusty friends I send you here,
With wishes hearty and sincere;
And if you raise their basket bed
You'll find some charming peeps outspread.   1156

55   This picture of the New Forest Foxhounds was taken at Longdown, just near Ashurst. They also met at Lyndhurst.

N.F. FOXHOUNDS
AT LONGDOWN.

56   A picture of the Old Farmhouse public house in Ringwood Road, Totton. Note the advertisement for Ashby's Brewery on the front of the building.

57   A somewhat deserted Lyndhurst Road, Ashurst. This is now the main A35 road to the well-known New Forest village of Lyndhurst, which attracts hundreds of visitors during the summer months.

58   A rather nice early advertising card for the New Forest Hotel at Ashurst. It was the main hotel in Ashurst and is still flourishing. Note the telephone number 33.

Telegrams:
"Sugden, Ashurst, Hants."   New Forest Hotel, Lyndhurst Road, R.S.O., Hants.   Telephone No. 33 Totton.
Station: Lyndhurst Road.

59   A splendid view of the front of the New Forest Hotel. I wonder if everyone posed for the photographer? It is still a very popular watering hole for horse riders today.

60   The Forest Inn, Ashurst.
It is one of the lovely old New
Forest inns, and still there on
the A35. This card is post-
marked August 1908.

61   Hounsdown, Totton. This small hamlet on the outskirts of Totton comprised a few houses, a shop and a pub. Apart from a large increase in traffic on what is now the main A35 road, the houses are little changed.

62   During the First World War there were several army camps scattered around the New Forest. This particular one at Ashurst was for Indian troops.

ASHURST CAMP

63   This is one of the few postcards in this series which pinpoints exactly where this First World War troop camp was in Ashurst. It fortunately shows what is now Ashurst Hospital in the background.

64 There was a very long series of photographs of these Indian troops at Ashurst; this is one of the more interesting showing the camp's shoe repairers at work.

ASHURST CAMP NATIVE COBBLERS

65   The Causeway Bridge, Redbridge. Note the signal box, long since demolished, but the Anchor Hotel is still very busy today.

The Causeway.   Totton.

66   Another card of the Causeway, Totton. This particular view seems to have been a favourite with the photographers. This card is one of the better ones clearly showing the Anchor Inn.

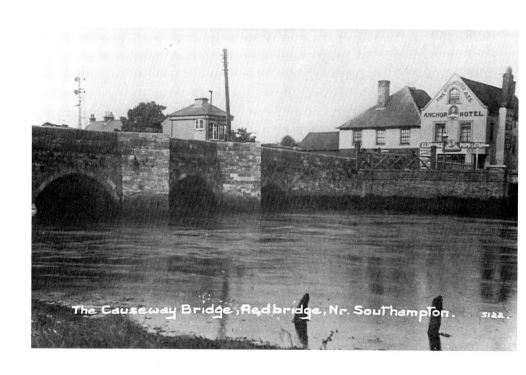

67   A peaceful scene looking towards Redbridge Causeway, showing the Anchor Inn and part of the famous reed beds.

68   A wonderful traffic-free view of the main street in Redbridge. The card is un-dated, but probably from the early 1900s.

69   The Ship Hotel, Redbridge. This was one of a
number of public houses in
Redbridge in the early 1900s,
most of them have now been
demolished, but the Ship Hotel is still there and serving
the local community.

70 Many picture postcards are 'lost' to their local area, because the photographer did not put a caption on the front. With this series though, the sender identified not only the location as being Redbridge Station, but also identified the individual soldiers and their regiment. This fine looking sergeant was Col. Sgt. J. Jefferson, E. Company, 7th Battalion, The Kings Regiment, Liverpool. The card is dated 1914. Further research has revealed Sgt. Jefferson was killed in action within months of this photograph being taken.

71 It would be interesting to know how many cards exist in this series of the 7th Battalion, E. Company. This picture seems to exude an air of unconcern by the soldiers for what the future might hold for them. The young boys seated on the ground were members of the 1st Totton Scout troop, but unfortunately they are not named.

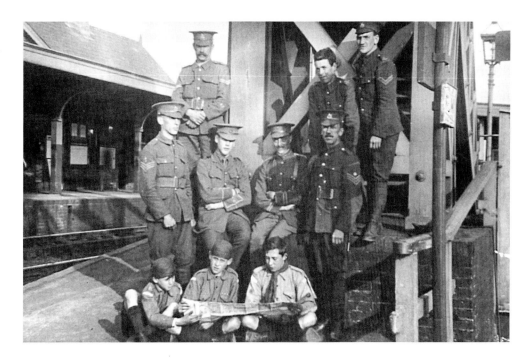

72   The Kings Regiment, 7th Battalion, must have had some spare time while waiting for their posting to the Front, they even managed a football match. For many of them it was to be their last ever game.

73   The 7th Battalion at Redbridge Station, expectantly waiting for their train to Southampton for embarkation to Flanders.

74 A final picture showing the 7th Battalion at Redbridge, entrained and waving farewell to the women and children on the platform. This photograph completely and poignantly catches the spirit of soldiers going to war in 1914.

75 The Netley Marsh and District Agricultural Co-operative Society Ltd. was originally built as a reformatory to house forty boys. It is now the premises of Gifford and Partners.

76   A wonderful view of Netley Marsh supply stores, about 1900. Netley Marsh is a small, but thriving village on the outskirts of Totton.